Dragonfly

Stephanie St. Pierre

H www.heinemann.co.uk/library

Visit our website to find out more information about **Heinemann Library** books.

To order:

☎ Phone ++44 (0)1865 888066

▤ Send a fax to ++44 (0)1865 314091

▢ Visit the Heinemann Bookshop at www.heinemann.co.uk/library to browse our catalogue and order online.

First published in Great Britain by Heinemann Library, Halley Court, Jordan Hill, Oxford OX2 8EJ, a division of Reed Educational and Professional Publishing Ltd. Heinemann is a registered trademark of Reed Educational & Professional Publishing Ltd.

OXFORD MELBOURNE AUCKLAND JOHANNESBURG BLANTYRE
GABORONE IBADAN PORTSMOUTH NH (USA) CHICAGO

Designed by Wilkinson Design
Illustrations by David Westerfield
Origination by Dot Gradations
Printed by South China Printing Co.

05 04 03 02   06 05 04 03 02
10 9 8 7 6 5 4 3 2   10 9 8 7 6 5 4 3 2 1
ISBN 0 431 01717 4 (hardback)   ISBN 0 431 01721 2 (paperback)

British Library Cataloguing in Publication Data

St. Pierre, Stephanie.
    Dragonfly. - (Bug books)
    1.Dragonflies - Juvenile literature
    I.Title
    595.7'33

Acknowledgements

The author and publishers are grateful to the following for permission to reproduce photographs:
Animals Animals, pp. 4, 18; Maria Zorn/Animals Animals, p. 5; Gary Meszaros/Photo Researchers, p. 6; Kim Taylor/Bruce Coleman, Inc., p. 7; Stephan Dalton/Animals Animals, pp. 8, 16, 25; Kim Taylor/Bruce Coleman, Inc. p. 9; Hans Pfletschinger/Peter Arnold, Inc., p. 10; G. I. Bernard/Oxford Scientific Films, p. 11; E. R. Degginger/Photo Researchers, Inc., p. 12; FLY D. NYM/Photo Researchers, Inc., p. 13; Stephan Dalton/Photo Researchers, Inc., p. 14; Dwight Kuhn, p. 15; Lynn M. Stone/Animals Animals, p. 17; Joe McDonald/Animals Animals, p. 19; Bruce Coleman, Inc., p. 20; Robert Armstrong/Animals Animals, p. 21; Bill Beatty/Animals Animals, p. 22; Kenneth H. Thomas/Photo Researchers, Inc., p. 23; Robert Lubeck/Animals Animals, p. 24; Corbis, p. 26; Joan Cancalosi/Peter Arnold, Inc., p. 27; John Gerlach/Animals Animals, p. 28; Rhoda Sidney/Photo Edit, p. 29.

Cover photograph reproduced by permission of Stephen Dalton/Animals Animals.

Special thanks to James Rowan and Lawrence Bee, for their help in the preparation of this book.

Every effort has been made to contact copyright holders of any material reproduced in this book. Any omissions will be rectified in subsequent printings if notice is given to the publisher.

Any words appearing in the text in bold, **like this**, are explained in the Glossary.

Contents

What are dragonflies?

Dragonflies are **insects**. There are about 40 different kinds in Britain. They got their name because they look like tiny dragons.

Dragonflies do not harm plants or bite people. They are useful because they eat bugs that harm people.

What do dragonflies look like?

Dragonflies can be green, blue or red. They have long, thin bodies and two pairs of wings. Some dragonflies are wider than your hand. Most dragonflies are the size of your finger.

Dragonflies have a mouth with sharp **jaws** for grabbing and eating other bugs. They have two big eyes and two small **antennae**. They have three pairs of legs.

How are dragonflies born?

Dragonflies lay eggs. Some lay their eggs in the water. Others use the stems of plants that grow near water. When the eggs **hatch**, the young live in the water.

The eggs hatch after about four weeks. The young are called **nymphs**. They are about the size of your eyelash. Dragonfly nymphs don't have wings.

How do dragonflies grow?

Dragonfly **nymphs** eat lots of mosquito **larvae** to help them grow. The nymphs have a special **jaw** that shoots out from their mouth to grab **prey.**

As the nymphs grow, they shed their
tight skin. This is called **moulting**. They
moult many times before they reach
adult size.

How do dragonflies change?

Finally the **nymph** is ready to change into an adult dragonfly. It climbs out of the water and onto a stem. It hangs on tight with its claws.

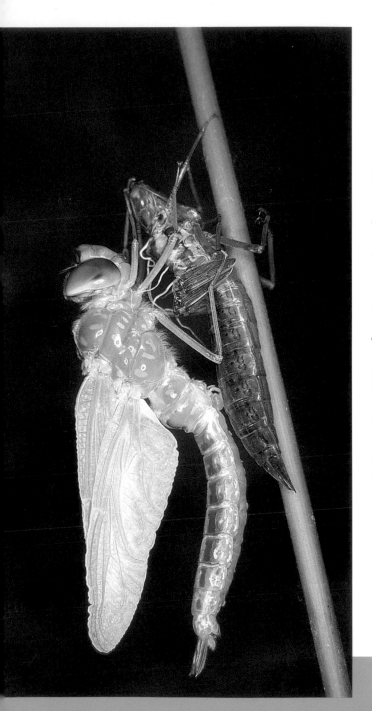

The nymph rests for a little while. Then it breaks out of its old skin for the last time. Now it has wings. It rests again while its body gets dry and hard.

What do dragonflies eat?

Dragonfly **nymphs** are **fierce predators**. They eat the **larvae** of other **insects**. As they grow bigger, they eat tadpoles and small frogs. They even eat small fish and **crustaceans**.

Adult dragonflies hunt while they fly. Their good eyesight helps them see other flying insects. Sometimes they hunt together to feed on large groups of smaller insects, like mosquitoes.

Where do dragonflies live?

Dragonflies live near streams, ponds, lakes, rivers, marshes and even waterfalls. There are dragonflies in most parts of the world where there is water.

Dragonfly **nymphs** live in water. Adult dragonflies have wings. They can fly a long way from water. They fly back to water to lay their eggs.

What do dragonflies do?

Dragonfly **nymphs** cannot fly. They live in water. They swim around the water plants, and hunt for their food. They sometimes lie at the bottom of a pond or lake.

Adult dragonflies fly very well. They can zig zag, turn and even fly backwards. They are also strong. They can lift things much heavier than they are.

How do dragonflies move?

Dragonfly **nymphs** breathe through **gills** inside their bodies. They move by shooting water through their gills. They can move faster than most creatures that live in the water.

Adult dragonflies use their two pairs of wings to fly. Before flying, dragonflies must sit in the sun, or shake and shiver to warm up the **muscles** in their wings.

How long do dragonflies live?

Most dragonfly **nymphs** live for a few years in the water while they grow. Adult dragonflies only live for a few months.

The most dangerous time for a dragonfly is while it changes from a nymph to an adult. It cannot fly or defend itself until its new wings and body are dry and hard.

Which animals attack dragonflies?

Birds and frogs eat dragonflies, if they can catch them. They catch the dragonflies when they are laying eggs, or when they are **moulting**.

Dragonflies can fly very fast. Usually they are too quick to be caught by birds or frogs. They can fly faster than you can run.

How are dragonflies special?

Dragonflies fly with great skill. They can perform tricks in the air that even helicopters cannot copy.

There have been dragonflies for millions of years. There are **fossils** that prove dragonflies are even older than dinosaurs. Some of those dragonflies were as big as owls!

Thinking about dragonflies

What must a dragonfly do before it is ready to fly? Why do dragonflies shiver?

This child wants to catch a dragonfly.
Do you think it will be easy or hard? Why?

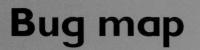

Bug map

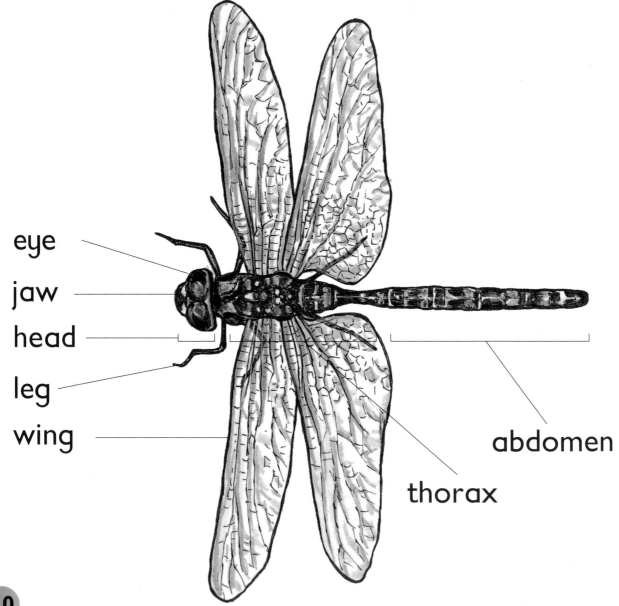

eye

jaw

head

leg

wing

abdomen

thorax

30

Glossary

abdomen stomach area, at the end of an insect

antenna (more than one are called antennae) long, thin tube that sticks out from the head of an insect. Antennae can be used to smell, feel, hear or sense direction.

crustacean relative of insects that has a tough shell. Woodlice, shrimp, lobsters and barnacles are crustaceans.

fierce frightening, strong

fossil remains left in stone, of animals or plants that lived a long time ago

gill part of the body that takes air out of water so that fish can breathe in the water

hatch a break out of an egg

insect small animal with six legs, and a body with three parts

jaw bony parts that make the shape of the mouth

larva (more than one are called larvae) baby insect that hatches from an egg and does not look like the adult insect

moulting shedding the old, outer layer of skin that has been outgrown

muscle parts of the body that helps it to move

nymph insect baby that has hatched from an egg and looks like the adult insect with no wings

predator animal that hunts and eats other animals

prey animal that is hunted for food

thorax middle, chest area of an insect's body, where the legs are attached

Index